IN THE KINGDOM
OF THE DITCH

IN THE KINGDOM OF THE DITCH

POEMS BY TODD DAVIS

MICHIGAN STATE UNIVERSITY PRESS • *East Lansing*

⊗ The paper used in this publication meets the minimum requirements of
ANSI/NISO z39.48-1992 (R 1997) (Permanence of Paper).

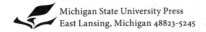 Michigan State University Press
East Lansing, Michigan 48823-5245

Printed and bound in the United States of America.

19 18 17 16 15 14 13   1 2 3 4 5 6 7 8 9 10

LIBRARY OF CONGRESS CATALOGING-IN-PUBLICATION DATA
Davis, Todd F., 1965–
In the Kingdom of the Ditch : Poems / by Todd Davis.
pages cm
ISBN 978-1-61186-070-2 (pbk.)—ISBN 978-1-60917-356-2 (ebook)
I. Title.
PS3604.A977I5 2013
811'.6—dc23
                                2012040825

Book design by Charlie Sharp, Sharp Des!gns, Lansing, Michigan
Cover design by Erin Kirk New
Cover image, *Burn Barrel*, oil on panel, 17″ × 16″ ©2009 Craig Blietz is used
with permission of the artist. All rights reserved.

g **green** Michigan State University Press is a member of the Green Press
press Initiative and is committed to developing and encouraging
INITIATIVE ecologically responsible publishing practices. For more information about
the Green Press Initiative and the use of recycled paper in book publishing,
please visit *www.greenpressinitiative.org.*

Visit Michigan State University Press on the World Wide Web at
www.msupress.org

In Memory of My Father
Dr. W. Harold Davis

&

For My Mother
Joyce Lee Davis

&

as always
For Shelly, Noah, & Nathan

CONTENTS

This is why we pray: we were not born tundra swans.

—K. A. Hays

Taxonomy

We've been taken captive
by the world, named by it, taught

to eat from its table. The whetted blade
slides through the flesh, thin veil

that parts to reveal what we think
is the soul. We set fires and burn

the earth because berry canes
won't come back without dirt

as dark as the color of its fruit.
Before the oldest trees were felled

we traveled the watercourse.
Now in the open fields we track

coyote, hoping to save the sweet
lambs we tend. Sadly, as night

stumbles down, all we find
are clumps of wool caught

in teasel's fine comb.
More than two centuries ago

Linnaeus began to arrange all
the names we've given back

to the world. This is how we know
black walnut hulls, when crushed,

smell like lemon, or when we walk
through sweet fern grouse will burst

into flight, dragging the plant's sharp
scent into the air. Near the stream

a tulip poplar blows down, leaves
turning the yellow of mustard

and ragwort. Despite the order
we've cultivated, the charts

we've set to memory, we're likely
to discover our way is one

of unknowing. When we die
may we be a pleasing word

placed in the mouth
of the world.

Perspective

How do you paint the color of bone, the pelvis where the flesh
has been cut away? For more than two days we've soaked in bleach
the ivory girdle of the deer my son killed. Every few hours I check
the bucket so I can watch the dissolution, the falling away of the life
that can't last. Think of O'Keeffe's inheritance. What her hands
were given by the skeleton of the world. What she was expected
to give back. Who doesn't want to hear a holy word echoing
along the rock's split lip? But to hunt means to stalk in silence, to listen
for the solace in an animal's missed step. Early on I learned
from my grandmother to fish is to search the sea by sending a line
down its length. When my sister caught the eel, we didn't know
what to do. The only other person on the bridge was a black man
seated on a five-gallon drum. He took the rod, laid it on the ground,
and in one stroke severed the head, held the dancing curve
until it slowed, then stuffed it in a bag. We slipped the hook
from between the teeth, ran our fingers across the ridges.
My sister peered through the cut hose and wouldn't tell me
what she saw. Today I stare at the shadows in the valley, see
what can be seen through the hole in the pelvis where the ball
of the femur should rest. The sky's different framed like this.
When there's nothing around it, it seems endless.

5

After Georgia O'Keeffe's "Pelvis with the Distance" (1943)

A Consideration of the Word "Home"

Because glass is more liquid than solid, because
this pane, made more than a hundred years ago, ripples

and bubbles, the prosody of its movement is like an epaulet
of stars shimmering on a night in August when the first

cool air is smuggled over the border and our vision
of what we thought was the unchanging world

grown fat with melons and the reddest peppers runs
floorward as we spy our father strolling within the arbor,

dreaming of the first hard frost and the dark fruit
that will turn sweeter as the vine withers.

Consciousness: An Assay

Black snakeroot goes to seed; black birch
litters the trail with yellow light. Trout

wrinkle the surface of the pond, curve back
into the premature darkness of deeper water.

We move toward absence: sound of wind
in leafless trees, the last dragonfly sliding

around our heads. To the left a pileated
woodpecker knocks on the door of a sassafras.

Whether we enter or stay doesn't matter:
doomsayers will continue their chant

about final things. Here it's the crease
in the ridge, the whistle of a red-tailed hawk

as the mind misses the fluting call of a hermit
thrush. The cord that binds us to this world

frays and unravels. Water continues to run
at the south end of the pond, endlessly

remade, a stream that falls away into the hollow,
persisting in its course before losing itself

in yet another stream. This is the way
of consciousness, the beginning

and the end, the alacrity of struck stone,
the drumming of a grouse as it breaks the air.

For Jane Hirshfield

Dona Nobis Pacem

The moon grows from nothing to a porcelain sliver.
The cat bloodies her feet against the screen chasing moths.

Our children sleep in the rooms above while I drag a cloth
across the red petals the cat leaves on the kitchen floor.

I join you in the bed of this passing hour, knowing
porcelain will again sift through the screen, and, again,

moths will flood to it: light cut by their beating wings,
which come morning our children will find in pieces.

Seeing Things

A 300-pound bear wandered into our village last April and ended up
trapped by a crowd staring at him as he moved along the main beam

of a maple in Mrs. Henderson's yard. The game commissioner drugged
and tagged him, took his sleeping carcass deep into the woods.

We don't have mountain lion anymore so bear try to lie down
with our children. On a logging road this past February a bobcat leapt

across the ruts in front of my truck—purple afternoon with nothing
moving, me thinking it might be the soul trying to escape

with my breath. I wish I'd gotten out of the truck and walked
in silence through the snow to see if this is how we're ushered

into the next life. But I couldn't hold my tongue, and the cat vanished.
The last few days the same bear has roamed near the stream

that runs behind my house. Hunger showed him the way back.
He'll wreck our bluebird boxes, feast on the orange and gold carp

in the neighbor's pond. The neighbor and I made a pact.
We don't plan on telling anyone about the bear

until he disappears with our children, and, then,
only after the apple blossoms fly away.

The Consolation of Wind

In the barn, as she helps her husband,
her belly bumps against the worn wood
of stanchions, the warm sides of cows
whose udders are tugged by rubber
and metal, whose milk runs the length
of the barn in a maze of plumbing.
She is tired and her back aches.
She uses fistfuls of bag balm
to ease the skin's stretching, child
kicking her insides as she shovels
manure and hoses the dairy parlor's
slick gutters. Like Perpetua
who was gored by a bull only to become
the patron saint of cows, this woman
is grateful for the neglected beauty
of bovine: fullness of breast, width
and curve of haunch, the strength
of sloped shoulders, the heavy eyes
that watch for the consolation of wind
as it rubs the limbs of lilac and dogwood.

For Craig Blietz

Limbo

What of those of us who are halfway here, almost
of this world, yet shuddering in the antechamber

of the pelvis, muscle pushing out against hands
that grab from below? And of those hoofed creatures

battering themselves against some tree to release
what they've carried into the yellow home of this day?

And the winged seed beneath the shell, offspring
who would do anything to be baptized into air?

What do we believe happens to those who remain
unborn, or, worse yet, live for only minutes?

The doe wags her bottom, fawn dangling from the red
jelly of her womb, while a coyote watches

in the dense laurel. When the heart begins
to beat for itself, there's no promise of salvation.

Every fall steelhead swim from open lakes
to the streams where they spawn in gravel beds—

tails fanning with passion that covers regret.
And my own child, unwilling to quit

his mother's body, even as forceps gripped
the sides of his head, doctor placing her foot

on the foot of the bed, yanking with such force
I thought he would tear in two.

Deer Dreaming Me

I have walked into the woods in darkness
and sit with my back to a black birch.

It has snowed the night before, then cleared,
so now cold works its way inside my coat:

unlaces my boots, sifts coarsely
against my throat. I have risen at four

the past three mornings and cannot keep
my eyes open as I dream of deer

coming down off the ridge, browsing
among moosewood and fox grape.

As they gather around me, my rifle rests
in my lap, left arm limp beneath it.

When I open my eyes they are gone,
yet I smell their musk, the pitched

heaviness of their breathing. Somewhere
deeper in the forest a doe dozes

under a hemlock, two others beside her.
Snow melts in a circle around their bodies

while inside her dream the woods grow quiet.
She makes the wind die down, checks to see

if I am in bed, asleep next to my wife, my rifle
safe in the corner room of our house.

Imago Dei

The weasel who lives
along the water's edge

splits the muskrat's vein:
jugular-blood stringing

the back of the head;
mouth shut until death's

jaw-hinge opens the throat
so tongue may lap warmth

and salt. What's left
of the idea we were made

in the image of God?
Stomach red with joy.

Ears raised to guard
against the approach

of another. Like the muskrat
our flesh comes undone,

and like the weasel-god,
our bloodlust is lost

in briar, or beneath
the dirt-roofs

of these muddy dens
we call heaven.

For Robert Wrigley

Midrash

*And the heart of man is a green leaf: God twists
its stem and it withers.*
—Nikos Kazantzakis

At first the hunger in his belly did not burn,
nor did it lie at the bottom with the heaviness

of stone. It was like iron hammered flat,
like the dull edge of a knife pushed against

a whetstone. Because hunger leaves no one
alone, as he passed a fig tree and found green

leaves but no fruit, he touched three limbs
and the tree withered. This did nothing

to sate his hunger, and like deadwood
catching fire, where there had been no heat

a blaze erupted, ravishing the air, until he
could not remember the taste of honey

and bread, the pungent bite of apple's skin,
and his scorched tongue hung from his mouth

like a stray dog no one will care for.
Those who followed asked why the fig tree

must suffer, why the flames of punishment
instead of love had fallen like a falcon

from the sky. Silence was the only answer,
and soon they slept by the fire. In his dream

he gathered from the dust stones the size of figs
and ate until he was full. He awoke to the sound

of water moving in a riverbed, the sweet drone
of bees flying among poppies. In the early dark

he went to the river's edge and drank deeply,
dousing the fire that had burned all night.

He then sent his disciples ahead to a village
where the sick lay on cots, their flesh like dates

laid too long in the sun. As he made his way
to that village, he departed from the road

to find a place that was hidden, and there
he shat out fig-stones, covered them with dirt

and blessings. In that place two trees sprouted
and bore fruit. Of this he told no one.

A Mennonite in the Garden

We staked and tied our tomatoes
like the woman in your poem
who had her tongue screwed

to the roof of her mouth, and like that
woman the tomatoes came to harm,
sacrificed to our hunger. Even our children

know Jan Luyken's etchings, the heft
of persecution, the reward of history's
painstaking script: Maeyken Wens

on a spit, flames rising from wood
cut and split by our own industriousness,
or Anneken Hendriks lashed to a ladder,

men trudging forward like mules, walking
the wooden staves until they stood upright.
With so much rain the fruit grows

too fast and too heavy, some of it
breaking the stalk without ripening.
Our neighbor's tomatoes have blight,

leaves wilted, so we collect the green
from our broken stalks, make relish
and bring it to their door.

Why couldn't those women have remained
untouched, somehow God leaving
the tomatoes unscathed?

The boy, who in my confusion, wanders
between these stories, plays a part
he never asked for: pear bestowed

through the dancing blaze, as if
forgiveness could conquer the anger
of such flames. We should know fire

isn't fastidious: fuel is fuel as it hisses,
then becomes ashes; soil in the garden
blacker for these efforts.

For Julia Spicher Kasdorf

Fishing for Large Mouth in a Strip-Mining Reclamation Pond near Lloydsville, Pennsylvania

The gills rake down the sides of his head, and the mouth
opens like the tunnels we used before the coal companies

hauled in dozers and trucks to scrape away the mountain
our grandparents had known. There was honor in riding

rail cars underground, something mythic as fathers said
goodbye to their children and traveled away from the sun.

Our teachers told us the story of Sisyphus, and we understood
how a stone might roll back upon the one who pushed it.

Most of the tunnels are gone, filled in or forgotten, holes
in our memory where the black line of money vanished

like the wind that sweeps over the backside of the Alleghenies.
As penance the state made us dig out this pond in the shape

of a kidney, water the color of liver, banks covered in cattails
and loosestrife. On the mounds of dirt that were left, goldenrod

grows in thin circles, like yellow mustard on bologna, the white
bread of cloudy skies balanced on the horizon where red oak

and hemlock should be. Black birch is the only tree
that comes up, rises toward the sun's lure, like a bass striking

the plastic popper my son dragged across the pond's surface, bait
imitating a frog's ragged dance, enticing this fish he hooked

and grips by the lower lip, both of them smiling, or grimacing,
or simply trying to hold still for the camera.

What Lives in the Wake of Our Sleep

I dream of peaches on the tree by the river,
of my youngest son lost along its muddy banks.

When I wake night's worry trails me to the bathroom
and later to the breakfast table. It is winter here

and the tree is bare. The peaches wait in the freezer
until my wife thaws them for cobbler. Each morning

my boy climbs the black steps of the school bus
and leaves me to what lies in the loose folds

of these sheets: the bed unmade, the mud untracked.

Two Sounds after an October Storm

The woods have changed: early wet snow
on leaves; torn limbs; entire trees on the ground.
Walking in to my hunting-stand, I scare up
two grouse from beneath a bent witch hazel,
an explosion of feathers as today's temperatures
are back where they should be. This time of year
bear continue to roam, eating acorns in the darkest part
of the hollow. After I killed my first deer, I couldn't stop
dreaming about how it died. I suppose that's as it should be:
to take a life is to live with that life until your own death.
This past week two bucks have been rubbing their antlers
against the slats of our deck railing. Even up high
on the mountain the red and white oaks are still green.
At 44 I'm not sure if I'm halfway to my death.

How many of us know what's coming when the first
heavy snow starts down? With this storm we stood
and watched, soaked through, until the woods began
to creak, and we walked out from under the trees
and into the field to wait for the first gunshot of beech
or maple breaking. Once it began you couldn't hear
the person next to you, and the sound of splintering
lasted most of the night. When we woke, the road
was closed, the power out. This is how it happens:
the throttled whine of a chainsaw; the faraway drone
of a single-engine plane surveying the damage.

Resurrection: A Field Note

In deep winter when the earth's mouth will not be broken
and the dead lay piled on the rough pine boards of the floor

in the barn, the moon cups its hands to catch its own light,
then turns palms down so the light washes over the rigid flesh

of those we say we have lost—(although we can see they simply
wait to be buried)—and in that light they rise up and walk

across these fields toward the houses they built, the gardens
they looked after. On such nights, what's left of our belief

in the world to come? Those we loved and quarreled with
open their mouths and sing, some even draw harmonicas

and penny whistles from their pockets. As they stride toward
the lives they spent their living on, spindled legs like mandolin

strings, only the remains of their voices float, caught by the wind
as they repeat the songs they learned by heart when their hearts

still labored beneath the sun.

Morning Poem

Blackberries hang in the darkest
creases of the trellis, each dimpled
to bursting. The black-eyed Susans
are mostly black, their yellow tresses
already rotted. Goldfinches wander
the air, meditate upon the coneflower's
sharp seed, trying to discern if it's time
to leave. This early, before anyone
has opened their doors, I watch chickadees
sidle up to sunflowers or hide in cosmos
while cricket song sifts through the screens
like fog in the belly of this valley.
I've been making jam most of the month,
and the jars from last night's batch

have been talking, lids sinking toward sweetness
with a satisfied metallic *ping*. The weatherman warns
of frost, so after the air warms this morning
I'll scoop the last bits of black from the canes'
green strings, bottom press the potato-masher
to render the berry syrup into a bowl
the color of nightshade. Other birds will dawdle
through, but none will be dressed as brightly
as the finches who helped greet the dawn.
If there's any consolation in the dying
we must do, then let it be stored on a shelf
in a raised glass jar, adorned with pictures
of strawberries and cherries, grapes and pears,
the pale seeds that fix in the cracks
of our teeth, floating in a sticky infusion
we lick from the ends of our breakfast spoons.

The Knowledge of the Lord

After the first snow
the tallest stalks of goldenrod
bed down in the far field.

The wind and the sun
the past few days
have erased the snow
so you might be tempted
to think the grasses
and those autumn flowers
laid down of their own accord.

Under the early dark
my boot grinds the dusty
flowerheads to seed
where they'll wait
for next summer's heat.

I like coming back
through the dark
when I can see you
moving in the light
of the window, setting
the table for dinner,
or helping our sons
with math.

As we grow older
the field on windy nights
sounds like the waters of a river
come to a narrows.

The Gospel of Beauty

Bees have made honey under the ribs of the dead, flown
from aster to goldenrod. The honey they spin is dark
and bitter despite its crystalline sugar. Little remains
yet skin's memory stretches across these bones, a cave
these bees congregate in like the earliest Christians
who hid among the catacombs, afraid to be found out,
afraid death might not offer the beauty of the honeycomb.

For Mary Rose O'Reilley

Brushwolf

When a man cocked a rifle and aimed at a wolf's head,
what was he trying to kill?
—Barry Lopez, *Of Wolves and Men*

It's no different here.
Mostly fear. Or hate.
Or some semblance
of failure.

If you grab the devil's
walking stick, it'll tear
your hand in two. Fruit
so heavy only a few
birds eat, and most
of the berries are left
to fall and turn the earth.

We believe the brushwolf
walks in shadows as dark
as that tree's fruit, blood
as acrid as rot in October.

Some nights you can hear
a fawn crying like a child,
torn and ragged, dragged
into death's quieting muzzle.

In the coldest months
we sit in hunting blinds
hoping for a deer to pass,
saying we must feed
our families.

At night we dream
beside our wives, praying
to the lie of sleep
that the innocence
of our children
might save us.

As we enter the hunt
our desire to see a brushwolf
rises: first wind after the sun
comes up; fire irrevocably
altering the earth.

But what of the wolf
that runs in our bodies?—
its blood a river
of silence wandering
this place we've cut
and cleared.

Each time we raise
our rifles, peer
into the undergrowth,
the head of the animal
is magnified, and the oldest
among us try hard
not to imagine
what we will kill.

Vigil

We stand over this child and watch the waters
roil, mud surfacing, bluebottle flies boiling
around ears, collecting at the seat of his pants.

This is the body we've made, sweet juice
of love's temptation, a split tomato: yellow
seeds in pink water. Like rain caught in a bucket,

like sunlight pushed flat against tin, I am trying
not to forget how our son spilled into the hands
of that first day. I suppose what's left is to settle in,

to listen to the mortal-song the body sings.
We shouldn't be surprised flesh chants as it does
the work of the body: rain pooling in spent cornfields,

small boy fluttering as if pinned to a clothesline.
Here's what we have left to learn: when the earth
drops away, we can't help but fall.

Letter to Dave B. with May's Insatiable Hunger Tagging Along

Most of the days have been full of green rain and clouds the color
of magnolia petals as they rot back into the emerging grasses. Three
weeks ago I planted half the potatoes (white Kennebecs), and just
Monday they broke the earth, a salad of leaves sprinkled with clay.
The other half (Adirondack reds) went into the earth yesterday. When
I stuffed my hand into the burlap sack to draw them out, I discovered
some had begun to putrefy. I'll bet the same will happen to us when the
hasp of our bodies is unbolted: old men wrapped in cloth, stuck in pine
boxes during the days of dogwood's white shining, the Judas tree just
past. Wouldn't it be nice to know that above our heads pink and yellow
lady's slippers slide gracefully out from beneath mountain laurel, the
world round like wild sarsaparilla's globe, spinning and spinning,
never really going anywhere new, yet full of vengeance and mercy and
the most foolish blessings of the new potatoes we'll harvest in July,
boiled, then mashed: a river of butter and milk, salt and sugar, the
bitter pepper that makes us gorge ourselves upon this one sweet life.

Upon Looking Down onto the Top of Your Head Where the Hair Has Gone White

Deep snows drape themselves

    like the long-loved, leg thrown over leg,

arm across breast, hand wandering

    the tunnels mink carve along the length

of the river where the ice is fluorescent

    and the last minutes of light are plum,

then crabapple, little warmth from this distant

    fire burning its way west to a place

of remembrance, of indwelling, of turning into.

Atrial Fibrillation

Yesterday was the dull gray of a river stone. This morning
snow covers our neighbor's roof, the sky the color of an indigo

bunting's cap. Fresh from sleep we reach back for last summer's
green, listen to a blue jay at the feeder as it cracks open a seed

to warm itself on the fire that still burns in the hull. To the west
our fields are bare, and beyond, in a room that holds her, my mother

wears a heart monitor. She rises stiffly from bed for a sponge-bath,
hoping her heart won't flutter like the wings of a sparrow, the furious

beating of a finch as it tries to bring the body into balance, an agreement
with the wind, the rhythm of the blessedly invisible air.

What We Do while We're Dying

All I can think about is what's going on
in my father's head as he rests in the hospice bed.
My grandmother would have said there were angels
hovering near, waiting to gather his soul. The morphine
pump kicks in every ten minutes, and with his head back,
the mouth gapes, showing us the space between his incisors.

When he could eat, which seems like a hundred years ago,
he'd take a bite of apple and separate the skin from the meat,
then push the red or yellow silk through the ivory fence
of his teeth. After this many days, I think that's what he's doing.
Chewing over his soul. Preparing to slip it through
the body's swinging gate.

Begging Bowl

Each night
the bowl
of our bodies
is emptied,
and as we wake
it begs to be filled:
resin of desire,
basin of water
into which we cup
our hands
and drink
and wash,
only to grow
thirsty and dirty
again: fingers soiled
and stained,
cherry's smudge,
grape's fleshy pulp,
so similar to a tongue
reaching after language,
after a sound equal
to this empty bowl,
this grieving bowl,
this body
we have faith
will wake
tomorrow.

Nurse Log

Bend back the bark of the world,
which is its skin, which is the way
we learn how veins carry blood
away from the heart, then back
into its echoing chambers. I'm tired
of hearing about the kind of men
who would kill me, the news of bombs
going off in endless loops on late-night TV.
In the forest above our house a fisher
stalks porcupines, and every so often
I find their torn bodies, once even
a corpse in the crotch of a white oak.
Its animal face lay open, empty and red
where the fisher's teeth had bitten down
to avoid the quills and to keep
the belly meat untouched. In nature
there is waste that good grows out of,
an abundance we are called to use.
In spring when we coax the bees
toward a new hive, Alverdia fetches
her wooden spoon and metal washbasin,
stands beneath the shad and pawpaw trees
whose blossoms the bees cover,
whose limbs sprout ten thousand wings,
and there she drums the basin
and hums a song she's made
for herself and for this swarm
that will follow her anywhere.
This isn't the news of the world
most of us live in. Two streams
meet in the floodplain where wet fires
of rot lap against fallen hemlocks.

Five seedlings have sprung up
along one of the logs, nursing decay
like piglets down a sow's length, or like
an infant in a desert village suckling
a mother's breast, oblivious to the murmur
of planes crossing overhead.

Thinking of Li Po while Fishing the Little J

I've known fishermen who have died
in the river, drunk on wine, trying
to embrace the moon's reflection.
I've known others fished out of the water

who cried after their own deaths
when the moon disappeared behind a cloud.
This evening, just before dark, the moon's
hand made rough brushstrokes on the river's

paper-surface, and trout, intoxicated
on green caddis flies, slept in an eddy
beneath the fallen body of a willow.
In their dreams these fish waited

for the wind to rise, for chokecherry
blossoms to be cast upon the water—
flowers purling around stone, as beautiful
and white as the hands of the dead.

What I Told My Sons after My Father Died

The emptiness of the catalpa flower's mouth opens
into nothing: stamen encased by cream.

My father called it a weed tree, despite his love
for the light it provided in June, the colors it caught

as dark came down over the garden we tended. The way
he told the story, after my great, great grandfather

escaped from a Confederate prison, he traveled north
by night along creekbeds. He rested beneath the draped

boughs of catalpa, drank branch water and ate pawpaws.
Supposedly in dark's false stillness he could tell the difference

between a hound and a groundhog, that in the water's hushed
movements he could pick out the stones breaking the surface

of the stream long before dawn woke those who hunted him.
In trying to explain the stillness, I don't wish to add

to my sons' sorrow. If I could play three notes
upon the fiddle, I'd do that instead. When my first boy

was born, in the nights after we brought him home,
I stood above his crib, head pressed over the rail

to assure myself he still breathed. I did the same
when I was a kid working at the animal hospital.

I'd open a cage, my ear flush with the chest
of a dachshund or Doberman and listen to the heart,

after the strain of surgery, as it settled back into a sound
like a kick wheel turning clay. My father taught me

the names for trees, which in turn I've taught my sons.
That's what it was like after he stopped breathing.

A bee disappears down the flower's mouth.
Although we can't see it, the bee's still there.

II.

Thoreau Casts a Line in the Merrimack

Pickerel, pout, eel, salmon, shad, even more
fish than these swim in the waters of the Self

where he casts again, hoping to catch, to feed,
to release some back into the river's current,

which runs from west to east, the watercourse
of our making, our perishing, mortal bodies:

the milling wheel that carries us over the bones
of the earth and allows us to flow outward

beneath the stars and the heavens, the other
rivers running through the glistening black.

Thoreau Hears the Last Warbler
at the End of September

Beneath the black gum,
whose leaves turn red

first, the light descends
and is changed: every cell

stained, skin polished
like stone, bathed

by the peripheral flight
of a migrant's song.

Dreaming the Dark Smell of Bear

Stop what you're doing!
      Put down your hammer and saw.
          What good is a cabin?

Look at bear's house: a hole
      in the snow where great puffs of lung
          rise through the roof of his dreaming.

Thoreau Considers a Stone

At the center of the pond an island of ice, circumference
twenty feet smaller than the pond itself. No wind or rain

so water clears, except where the sun pushes the ice's shadow.
This man, unsure of the pond's depth, throws a stone,

weight puncturing its plane, the slow drift in sluggish water.
The life of a stone is lost, or, at best, ignored, but this man

returns to his hovel to record the sound a stone makes
when it pierces the frozen mask. That night he considers

how in time all masks disappear, and, with this, how all things
expand or shrink. In his sleep he dreams of light pressing down

to reveal the stone: a turtle, no longer asleep, rising toward
new air, hind claws making use of that very stone.

Emptying the Bedpan

He only uses this basin in the coldest
months, when rising from bed
and out the door seems less bearable
than a full bladder. In winter
he drinks little, mostly snowmelt,
and his urine smells strong
like the hemlock boughs he lays
his head upon. Before making
breakfast, he opens the front door
and pitches the golden sap to the left
of the path, which last night
was roofed by snow. Come spring
nothing will grow in this spot, unless
more rain than wanted falls, floods,
forgives this man's nightly indiscretion
and reminds him in warmer months
to walk farther along.

Give Us This Day

July and the ink
of blackcap raspberries
splatters ditches
and clear-cuts: green
banks singing, my tongue
rocking inside my mouth.
Who blessed by this dark
sugar could stay quiet?
Ants wander drunk
into my bucket, across
the visible world
that feeds us, that makes
an offering each day:
beach plum or pawpaw,
morel or puffball, even
the spider-legs
of purslane
and the sharp
bite of sorrel.

For Mary Oliver

48

Psalm Written the Last Week of December

These motions everywhere in nature must be the
circulations of God.
—Henry David Thoreau, 29 December 1841

Praise the ice storm, the world glistening and undone.
Praise the ridge, the freeze and thaw split the stone.
Praise the sound of such undoing, the scarves of bodies
adrift and swaying. Praise the boards and roof that hold.
Praise beauty for loss, for what we make from what we lack.
Praise swamp, cardinal's wing on alder branch. Praise
raven's song and chickadee's lisp. Praise pickerel and perch
beneath the floe. Praise fox's trail, a sounding line
through the household of water, moon, and snow.

Thoreau Dreams of Margaret Fuller
Three Days after Her Death

He finds himself staring across the shoals of Fire Island, her body
beneath the waves, beneath the crown of a crescent moon, the coinage

of its inconstancy. Her child has already been rolled in the surf, buried
in the clutched arms of a dead sailor. The sea refuses to give up

her body, as she refused to try for the shore while the ship came apart
beneath her. He wonders if she knew this was a thin place, a space

of rest, or if it was simply the sea's seduction that laid her patience?
The water has stolen her words: the manuscript's shell

and the winged figure of love raging for vindication. He knows loss
is human, as is the desire to place blame, to find meaning in death,

to weep forever if the body of the beloved is lost, never to be lowered
beneath dirt's rim. In the dark there is always the risk we will run

aground, sandbar tossing us from our bunks, heaving the stern
and bringing freight crashing through the vessel's side.

Before he arrives nearly a thousand people comb the wreckage,
weigh the planks and spars, stealing away boxes shipped

from the old world to this new place where a woman might conjure,
might possess the idea, all things being equal, that the ballast

could right the ship, that night might allow it to sail safely
into harbor.

In the Clear-cut

Saws have flown recklessly like hummingbirds among honeysuckle,
and two days ago the powder mill burst in flame: wreckage

of blackened limbs, severed heads and singed skin.
We take arms against nature while the machinery of our despair

is fed by desire. Stumps circle the pond, marking our departure,
as we push farther into the West, the world forever opening

before us. To our surprise we find in hand the hardwood
of peavey hooks, our feet braced on clotted rivers, where we ride

the water with a brave ignorance. None of us knowing
how little our deaths depend upon any rule of our own devising.

The Virtues of Indolence

Gray birch sprawls
next to footbridge;
stream talks on and on.

Five snakes ring the tree's
limbs, stretch and sleep
away morning.

The bureaucracy of water
can't stop them; they ask
no permission for taking
such ease.

In July's heat freedom
hangs from these branches,
like hair come undone
or fingers trailing
across a leaf.

Offering, as One Example, the Satisfaction of the Bee

Sun slowly burns the gray tissue
of morning, and bees, who spent
the night beneath the long flower
of goldenrod, sway with the stalk's
movements, stiff with cold and fog.

Yesterday a red-tailed hawk lifted
from a tamarack to take a rabbit,
and on this walk I find owl pellets
near a downed oak: the torn limb
of a warbler, the discarded head
of a shrew.

These are the beautiful deaths
of usefulness. Imagine your life
taken to feed another, your very
being consumed in the belly's
furnace, awaking to heavy
wing-beat as you fly above
the tallest spruce.

The best we can hope for
is to scatter our selves
across the darkest parts
of the earth: rain relinquishing
these late flowers and our passing
love, which too often lusted
only for the self, forgetting
the sweet tenacity of the bee,
the waxen comb of delight.

Thoreau Surveys the Ice

*Sometimes, also, when the ice was covered with shallow
puddles, I saw a double shadow of myself, one standing
on the head of the other, one on the ice, the other on the
trees or hillside.*
—*Walden*

In late March he tromped over rotting snow, hardened
edges, knee-high holes that held the leg until the weight
of want and momentum broke through to the next,
and the next, which led to the pond's scalloped ledges,
the distance between piled winter and spring's wanton
wedge. He came with wool blanket, with smoking branch,
and built a fire, fed it, listened for the whip-crack
of heaving ice. He did not sleep because he had come
to see the ice undone, to witness winter's end, its weight
pushing what little ice remained to the pond's dark bottom,
to the cold springs, which in summer thrust
beneath swimming feet, to the self's double-shade
who skates on ice, then, as if lost, plunges deep
into spring's first floral green.

In the Kingdom of the Ditch

where Queen Anne's lace holds
its saucer and raspberry its black

thimble, the shrew and the rat snake
seek after the same God,

who mercifully fills the belly
of one, then offers it to the other.

Heaven Come Flying

They move through the trees like wind
or light, and like light or wind

they will not stay. By tomorrow
the songs of these birds will be absent,

and the light will not be yesterday's
but today's. The leaves will not make

a sound, and I will wonder if wind
ever shook this place, if the bright bodies

sang or foraged or filled the canopy
in numbers so dense you might believe

heaven was something to see, to feel
flying fast near your face.

Thoreau, in Death

All April stone weeps, and high, thin clouds ask
how we will know when the spirit has left the body.

Even now he recognizes where he is. He says he must
walk through one world at a time. Because he cannot

see the plum and pear trees from his bed, he questions
if they still bloom. He thinks he hears a veery

among the new leaves, remembers gazing up
through limbs to see the movement of their throats

in song. Those who have gathered smell the heavy
pollen of pitch pine and recognize that leaving

is no different than entering: we can't take with us
what we hope to remember. Before the door

to the room is shut for the night, he repeats
what he knows will be lost—first, *moose*; then, *Indian*.

Consecrated

Eight ravens roost
in a grove of sumac,
burnt horns offering
no warmth
to these black-cloaked
monks whose vespers
echo against
the cabin's roof.

III.

Not Writing, Then Writing Again

Days and days away from words:
only silence and the body's movements.

No B-film horror, lips sewn together, tongue
lopped off and lugged behind with a rope.

A simple attempt to live beyond language:
hovel built of branches, head laid upon hemlock.

The hope this is enough for a world that cannot
be bound by a word. Then a ring

around the moon: not the small ring that holds
rain, but an enormous circle: fire's holy

indulgence as it rises out of the forest
and at last offers a reason to speak.

Hermetic

The man walks into the woods with a rifle on his shoulder,
says nothing to the boy who has followed him there. For safety

the chamber is empty: bullets in the breast pocket of his jacket.
After more than five hours listening to the sound of limbs

with no leaves, they hear a deer picking her thin legs
through windfalls and the striped canes of moosewood's

last growth. The man presses the line of a finger to his lips,
and the boy puts gloved hands over his ears as the noise

of black powder and metal disappears. The woods dissolve
into a different quiet than before, and the man tells the boy

to stay in the stand while he goes to the animal's side.
Because the body lies askew, he places her twisted legs

beneath the torso, brings her head back to true, and before
the knife relieves the body of its burden, bends to the hole

the bullet has made, whispers into the growing circle of blood
a prayer to be forgiven for all the things he cannot pray.

Hawks Flying

Stone is only one of the excesses of God,
and it is through stone some of us know
God. To gather stone against the ocean's
coming is to say water and sky may enter.
Stone perched on stone: a window
through which we glimpse the world
to see hawks flying and to forget
we are human. We know what we build
cannot last. Even the stones will become
rubble when the hawk's eyes blacken,
and hunger's shadow drowns the words
we've placed in the mouth of God.

After Robinson Jeffers

When the Body Is Absent

The light that lifts the day has fallen on beebrush, and the ghost
of God, which smells so much like these pale flowers bees cross over,

is everywhere in the air. The stars disappear one by one, and once
again we are blind to what anchors the body: peeling bark

of madrona tree, thorn of honey mesquite, purple dust of cenizo
settling in dry basins as the sky opens to another shade of blue

and the sun to another shade of white.

Coal

The bottom of the world

    and the sounds that reside there.

The music beneath the sounds

    beneath the world.

Because I can't tell where the world begins

    and we end, I keep the house cold,

knowing to burn the lamp is to change

    the insides of the mountain to ash.

We're told that to repent means

    to turn around: like a bulldozer

scraping the edge, like the darkness

    of slurry against a dam,

like men running in a shaft of light

    as the black seam catches fire.

For Harry Humes

Three Songs for Flannery O'Connor

I. THE GIRL WHO TAUGHT A CHICKEN TO WALK BACKWARDS

Mostly she loved hens whose necks grew
too long, curved like gourds, crooked combs
that toppled over the sides of their docile heads.
At school when she was bored she stared
at the boy with the wrecked chest, whispered
in his spoon-shaped ears that it was easy to catch
a hen and teach it to walk backwards, strutting,
even dancing with an oblong gait. After the boy's
grandpap ran over his leg, drunk and backing down
the drive, he walked with crutches, later with a limp.
In *Ripley's* she'd read of a rooster who lived
thirty days with its head cut clean off. She told him
she worried about that chicken's sorrow, its grief
at not being able to peck. She supposed the boy
had to hide his secrets, like a hatchet's head buried
in a stump. Eventually all birds were beheaded:
the family's cook grabbing the flightless bodies,
thrusting them into boiling water, then plucking,
plucking, plucking. Whenever the boy tried to speak
it sounded like a hen's clucking beneath his peach
moustache, which was the same color as the sky
at dawn when she coaxed her hens with meal,
even molasses. Instead of letting the birds aimlessly
scratch, she'd shove her hands into apron pockets,
thrust her head forward, and march straight
as a newly plowed furrow, her stride narrow
as the path to heaven. Upon her approach
what chicken wouldn't take a step back?
The day the news crew arrived to film the bird
the boy came riding on his bike: hair standing up

like wind in a coxen comb, sternum like a chicken's
breast sticking out from under his white-pressed shirt.
She took his hand because she already understood
at some point we must take a step backwards
to see whether we're frying in the fat of our sins,
or whether love, when we try to own it, must become
beautifully misshapen.

II. NOODLING BLUES

At the bottom of the river, arm under the belly
of the bank, water cuts away sycamore roots
and his hand slides easily into the channel cat's
mouth, until it realizes he is the bait *and* the hook,

then swings its tail along the river's bed, reeling
silt, water little more than mud, what was murky
made blacker, and what he thought he held
now holding him down, shaking the last

of the breath left in his chest, which he tries
to hang onto until the other two in the boat
take the long hook to the fish, bring it caterwauling
over the bow, his hand still half way down the gullet

and all of them wrestling the river's current, grabbing
at air and water, gasping in a howl, the three of them
gaping at what's written across the fish's face
just after the hammer crushes its skull.

III. IN THE BACKSEAT

The warmth of the girl's inner parts, the place
her momma says the Holy Ghost resides, is wet,
and this boy who kisses her with his mouth thrown
open, as if he were about to laugh, has his hands
inside her blouse, nearly inside her heart.
She wonders if as he raises her skirt, as he tosses
her legs up high against his shoulders, if God's
own spirit will come flying out, never to return;
if all she'll be left with is what her biology teacher
calls *genitals*; if when she pees in the outhouse
the flies will know the difference.

Theophany

In the August heat of Rutherford, New Jersey,
Doctor Williams grasps a baby as its head
crowns, black-haired, slicked with blood
and feces, tipping out onto the plump white

thighs of the woman who cleans houses
on the street where he lives. With the sharpest
scissors he can find, he clips the line that leads back
to the abandoned lot where Queen Anne's lace

gathers at summer's end, flowers rounded
to the fullness of a cheek, a forehead stroked
and kissed, a mouth opened to accept most any
gift, like the ice from the icebox that melts

upon this woman's tongue as she sleeps with the baby
between milky breasts, the crying finished for now,
and the doctor's hands pushing loose strands of hair
from the poem of her face.

Ordinary Time

After fiery tongues. After wind all night. After we've said

we're sorry. This is what's left. Disheveled hair from fitful sleep.

Hunger for toast and jam. Tea with milk clouding its surface.

Sons off to school and the house lost to quiet.

Clock on the mantle silent. Key on the sideboard to wind it.

Spring Melt

Water remakes
what was made
before and reforms
itself in the bed
of its own making.

Its surface reflects
cherry blossoms,
moon's ivory
cut and placed
at petal's edge.

See the floating bridge:
how it always moves,
how we dip our fingers
in this very spot
yet touch the sea.

The Sound of Sunlight

On the far side
of the canyon
light
is burning
through two
draws
like water
rushing
into an empty
riverbed.

A canyon wren
opens
her mouth
and a coyote
stops
midtrail
before vanishing
among juniper.

As we descend
the eastern wall
we look
down
onto
ponderosa
pine
and witness
the shadow
of a merlin
chase

the merlin
itself.

Behind us
in the meadow
where we lay
last night
the squall
of an elk
picks up
the sound
of sunlight
and joins it
in a flood
of bugling.

Letter to Dave B. from the Karen Noonan Center on the Chesapeake Bay

The last two days out on the bay I observe tundra swans leaving the flat horizon of this water, arcing over tidal pools and the inescapable prairies of marsh grass. You're on your mountain to the north, closer to their calls as they wing their way away from this estuary that saves them each winter. After so many months of shifting land, of rising and falling tides, their heavy bodies must ache for release, a reprieve to our comings and goings, whether by boat or air or, oddest of all, by car, which looks nothing like the way these birds travel. It's the unyielding tundra where they'll give themselves over to their own desires. I suppose most of us need the solid earth beneath our feet as we choose a mate. The undulating waters of the heart make it hard to remember which flyway to follow: how to spend these transitory days in the half-light of summer, brooding over what we've made between us.

Last of the Sea

Gull's eye, dart-pupiled, ringed-
red, bulges as the bird gorges
on half-dead fish: throat straightened
to heave the head further down
the gullet. When the tide goes out,
we're left with brackish muck,
the smells of gut-piles as we clean
our catch, open our mouths, and shovel
the last of the sea into the ravenous
caves of our bellies.

After Jamie Wyeth's "Gluttony" (2005)

Missing Boy

I do not
want my son
to enter
the den
of sorrow.

At sixteen
he already
knows
too much
of the world.

Like a pine
snake,
he slides
toward his
burrow,
leaves behind
the skin
of his former
self.

It sloughs
and curls,
scales
of what
he's learned
but now believes
he does not
need.

Apophatic

The mind is murky, mottled
from too many days of rain.
I miss the thrush's fluting
and realize it's not the earth
that's dying but my attachment
to it. The first writing
was on the body, then the skin
of trees—pokeberry crushed
and driven to ink. The fox's
track is delicate, and where the river
rose and spilled, it left an unreadable
script. What does it mean to take
something you've not been given?
In the dream evening primrose
blooms the first yellow of a broken
vessel, juniper like the olive
skin of those animals we christen.
The rattle of the catalpa pod opens
into sleep while in the orchard
I gaze up at red planets adrift in space.
Does the doe dream of this place?
And the dog whose hind legs twitch
in sleep as he gives chase?
The field beyond the orchard
lies fallow, and orange and black
beetles devour milkweed,
laying eggs that will hatch
on the undersides of leaves
long after their deaths.

For Chris Dombrowski

Most of What Is Written Is Simply Grief

Three months
after his father's death
he enters the woods
with his own sons
and walks the path
that rises above
the river.

Even after
they've climbed
more than a mile
they can hear water
on the hollow stones
below.

For a time
they sit, and he tries
to tell them
about the sparrow,
about the number
of hairs
upon their heads.

They say nothing
on the trek back
to the car,
and at home
they pick burrs
from their socks
and boot laces.

Heliotropic

In the evening light the dove's undersides
look yellow, and the bush that grows along
the porch has flowers red as a tanager's back.

At dinner hummingbirds come to press needle-
beaks into trumpet-blossoms, the music
of their work drowning our conversation.

Why would anyone forsake this gospel of beauty?
Consider the bees covering the heads of sunflowers,
the sunflowers turning to follow the light.

When the world is pink, and the sun has begun
to sink to the other side of the earth, we walk
into fields tall with goldenrod to pick the daisies

my grandmother called moon-pennies, until the dark
makes it hard to see, and we must search for the light
glowing in the windows of the house to guide us home.

The Poet Stumbles upon a Buddha in Gamelands 158 above Tipton, Pennsylvania

A young boar (*Ursus americanus*) rests his rump

      on the pliable beam of a devil's walking stick, bending

the tree halfway to the ground so he might claw black

      and purple pebbles from its crown into a mouth as large

as a bushel-basket, tongue turned dark as the sweet scat

      he leaves in the middle of the path, a host of berries

littering his belly, and his great head reared back

      in a grin, no concern for abundance or waste or

for what comes after this early September light,

      which filters down through yellow poplar leaves, wind

making a sound like temple bells caught seventy feet up

      in the canopy.

           For David Shumate

Crow Counsels Me in the Ways of Love

Crow comes to the garden, lands
near the largest cantaloupe, proceeds
to walk back and forth, head shaking
from side to side. Crow talks incessantly
while I pick weeds from around tomato vines,
the leafy tops of turnips, the oblong peppers
that touch the earth like fallen breasts, or
a drooping cock. Crow says rain will fall
this afternoon, suggests I wait to weed:
wet earth makes such work go with ease.
In his torn voice Crow is forever
giving advice. Last week, after fighting
with you, Crow counseled me, said to pick
a cup of raspberries, to lay them in a circle
atop your bowl of cereal.

Deposition

Five ravens lift from sumac
the color of a blood orange,

and I wonder what's to be seen
in flight's dark hand. There's no sky

as clear as this. A spray of blue
at the start of September, leaves

on the ground to reveal the last
of the wild cherries. I used to think

the fruit too bitter, rough as the song
the ravens sing. With bloated skins

and black seeds run through piles
of scat, I'm beginning to reconsider.

That first judgment was made
by someone younger, his only desire

to fill the belly, to satisfy the burning
ache every boy feels. Death, a far-off

and awful dream, only made sweeter
the meat of plum or peach. Neither lust,

nor its sidekick death, have vanished yet,
so like the fisher who takes his sweet time

to scour this section of woods, I'll allow
one or two, perhaps as many as three

of these sour stones to sit on my tongue:
drift of time gathering the rank juice

at the back of my throat. With my father
spread across the earth, I'll sing

for the ravens return, sing into the world
an old refrain to waken to the place

near the middle of the river
where water plunges over granite,

where most mornings I kneel
with eyes wide open, trying to pray

without ceasing.

Perigee

A cold end to January and the moon is as close to us
as it's going to get: river sluggish where ice forms
at the edges of exposed rock. Not far from here
a friend found the first shed of the season. I imagine
the buck in the floodplain, aimless with only one antler.
All things move from balance to imbalance, and for the past
three hours two horned owls have been piping a song
that seems heavier on one side. Last week I found pellets
in a circle as broad as a pie pan. (Does the moon's light
cast from this distance make it easier for these birds
to hunt?) Somewhere in the shadowed trees above our house
a shrew scurries in and out of the hollowed body of a maple,
every few feet stopping to look for the owl's shadow.
Frost rings the window as I listen to night's traffic: coyote
on the hill above the dam, these owls who never seem to tire,
the timid deer scuffing at the base of a red oak in search of acorns.
What can we really know? Illumination is a beautiful word,
made even more lovely by this moonlight on our bed, outlining
the curve of your back, your strong legs curled
beneath the white blanket.

Somnambulance

All the sleepers who rise from their bodies and peer down
at the sheets and blankets that cover them leave a cast
of their slumbering, shadows where their heads pushed deep
into pillows. In what way will we know if we have loved God?
Like Lazarus, the dead are wrapped in sheets, buried in night-
clothes. The living enter sleep the same way. In the morning
may we rise and pray when we hear the voice of the one we love.
May the stench of death be washed from our mouths. May Christ
not weep for what lies ahead: whether grief, or simply
some long awaited sleep.

Transfiguration

When I walk among the beech saplings that rise from the roots
of the mother-tree, each turns in a cord of light and I imagine
this is what we mean to say when we speak the word *God*.
On the ridge above Three Springs Run, I think of my wife,
how it's been more than a decade since we loved furiously,
coming together at any hour, lust for a child of our own
driving us to such desire. Last winter while snowshoeing
I saw a deer among the rhododendron lunge against
the deepest snows, belly weighed by the life she carried, fixed
midstep, leg stopped halfway to the ground, struggling
to make it to the emerald and blue of summer into which her child
might run. As a teenager I worked with my father
at the animal hospital, hands covered in blood, pushing aside
lungs and intestines to get a better look at the blossoming tumor
he would cut from the dog's chest, the fine handwork of his sutures.
When my wife allowed me to enter her was it God or me
mumbling the come-cry, the startled relief that love and lust
are the same in such moments? The radiant air and the singing
of the flesh as it does the work of the body is why Christ climbed
the mountain, made three dwelling places: the first for birds
at play in the air; the second for fish in the coraled sea; the third
for our own feet which cling to the hard rock of this earth.
When we enter the world at birth, arms flailing at the unexpectedness,
lungs gasp after breath and throats constrict against the first
mouthful of milk. Scientists tell us as the earth warms
the gaps in the ice floes will run like rivers, freshest water
poured into the sea. No one is anointed by such melting,
yet the beauty of glistening ice, its dissolution, can't be denied.
In October cancer root blackens and the goshawk flees.
Below the blueberry field where giant chestnut trees once stood
leaves turn the sharp red of a scattered death and pignut hickory
and black birch wrap themselves in golden scars as everything

is transformed. To be human is to know illumination can't last.
Canary grass shines in the fallen sunlight of late day, reflects
our desires, burnishes and buries them deep in the marsh.
Against the coming dark we collect wood cast aside
in the windstorm, build a fire for warmth, for what light
we might offer to those who follow after.

For David James Duncan

Last Bones of Winter

Where the snow drifted deepest
I find the last of it hiding beneath stone.

Soon wood sorrel will blossom, white
as the snow it replaces. What else does death mean

except *not here now*? In the new warmth
the plum tree fills its branches with pink

bags, and near the seep skunk cabbage crawls
from its grave. Somehow my father knew

he would disappear before the last of the year.
In this new time without him the pear

tree's white wings beat, then fly, leaves
unfolding the second week of May.

The apple tree sends its flowers into the river
even sooner, and I realize I don't ever want

to *not be here*. I suppose that was true for my father
as well. Every year there comes a night when the last

bones of winter vanish, when temperatures
stay above freezing and stone settles deeper

in snow's absence. On such nights the flesh
can't help but fail, falling away and collecting

in the turning grass, only to become
something else.

Umbilical

As far as the eye will take you it's honeysuckle and cedar,
skeleton of last fall's teasel and this spring's pasture.

From the height of the narrows where the crease comes
down into the valley redbud flows over broken rocks,

and later in May the flowering cones of black locust
cloud the basin floor. Black Angus bent in supplication

to hunger hear the echo of our voices as we ascend
the ridge, wishing one another a sweet Sabbath

and our own gladness at having yet one more day
near the navel of this blessed world's unraveling.

Poem on the Anniversary of My Father's Diagnosis with Pancreatic Cancer

The vertical stripe of aspen wrinkles the dense green
of the understory with one of the eighty major shades
of white. Ferns clump around this light at the base
of the tree, and I wish it would brighten the center
of my chest where the rhythm has been off-kilter
for the past year. How odd it seems that happiness
can skitter away into the small door along the baseboard
of the body, a cartoon mouse chased by a cartoon cat.
I'm still getting smacked with the oversized mallet
of my father's death, and it sounds like a pileated
woodpecker hammering at my ears. I hear the stream
the topo map showed somewhere in the rhododendron
grove toward the bottom of the ridge. I'll likely find
beneath those fronds a cardinal flower, wet and fecund.
No doubt spend some time watching its own particular
delight *drip, drip, drip* like a faulty faucet, the continuous
play of water carrying all our abstractions—beauty, joy,
sorrow—down to the Chesapeake Bay and on out
into the heavy undercurrents of the Atlantic.
Don't tell me this plant doesn't feel ecstatic at the way
it's adorned. No one dresses in drag without a smile.
Even if you bite your tongue, blood's gift of salt remains.
Off to the left a cerulean warbler shuffles its sheet music,
sends a shaft of light into my aging brain, which as it turns out
is better than if my chest had been cracked open to insert
a pacemaker. Whitman was right about the body
being electric, but after this past year
I don't assume anything anymore.

A Prayer for My Sons, after a Line of Reported Conversation by the Poet William Blake to a Child Seated Next to Him at a Dinner Party

If I could send the sun
sprawling from my mouth,
if each night the moon might drop

from my eyes onto your head,
if I could reach up and take a star
whose light has traveled toward you

for thousands of years and place it
under the bed where you sleep,
I would do all these things. But

being a man who has seen
no angels and who at times doubts
what he's been told in church,

I'll simply ask what the Poet asked—
that God would make this world
as beautiful to you as it has been to me.

For Brian Doyle

Meditation on Hunger at 2 A.M.

Night is the black earth in the garden, a peach
held to the sky as the moon writes the history

of its shadow on the bedroom floor. Awake,
I remember cherries in a white bowl and think

of the faces of those I have loved
rising to the surface of the pond

where I fish with my sons. The flesh fades
if not fed; this is the business of living.

In his dying my father taught me language
fails. Thus, his love for the turnip's sting,

even when soaked in butter and cream,
or the sweet on sweet of honey drizzled

over baked apples, makes an elegy
of autumn olive as it takes over this field.

How could it be otherwise, and what choice
do we have? Like him I give thanks

for the neighbor's draft horse, asleep
and dreaming in its stall, enormous teeth

moving over oats that still sit in a scoop,
waiting for a hand to offer them.

I'll Catch You Up

I'm in the upper field again
where rock fell
and the sky opens.
No trees grow here.
Deerberry hangs its pitch
black fruit like lanterns
carrying bits of night
into daylight.
It's always the opposite
that illuminates: your being
dead, me alive; my presence
in this field, your absence; the sun
in September, the coming dark
of December. Don't worry.
I'll catch you up. After I sit
a while with the dark pith
of berry bittersweet
on the tongue, I'll continue
down the old logging road
that leads toward the spring
that runs along the bottom
of the ridge.

Acknowledgments

My thanks to the editors of the following journals or publications in which these poems first appeared, sometimes in different form.

American Literary Review: "Two Sounds after an October Storm"

The American Poetry Review: "The Poet Stumbles upon a Buddha in Gamelands 158 above Tipton, Pennsylvania"

Appalachia: "Give Us This Day," "Heaven Come Flying" (as "Thoreau Listens for the Warblers"), and "The Virtues of Indolence" (as "In Praise of Indolence")

Artful Dodge: "Coal"

Atlanta Review: "The Sound of Sunlight" and "Heliotropic"

Blueline: "Atrial Fibrillation" and "Most of What Is Written Is Simply Grief"

Chautauqua: "The Knowledge of the Lord," "Limbo," "Missing Boy," "Perigee," "Seeing Things," and "Transfiguration"

Christianity and Literature: "Last Bones of Winter"

Cold Mountain Review: "Morning Poem"

Connotation Press: An Online Artifact: "Thoreau, in Death" and "In the Kingdom of the Ditch"

Crab Creek Review: "Not Writing, Then Writing Again" and "Ordinary Time"

Ecotone: "Nurse Log"

Ekphrasis: "The Last of the Sea"

5 AM: "A Prayer for My Sons, after a Line of Reported Conversation by the Poet William Blake to a Child Seated Next to Him at a Dinner Party"

Flyway: "Spring Melt"

Folio: "Resurrection: A Field Note"

The Fourth River: "Hawks Flying"

The Hampden-Sydney Poetry Review: "Apophatic" and "I'll Catch You Up"

Image: "Midrash"

The Journal: "Fishing for Large Mouth in a Strip-Mining Reclamation Pond near Lloydsville, Pennsylvania"

Kestrel: "Deer Dreaming Me"

Natural Bridge: "Taxonomy"

Naugatuck River Review: "In the Backseat" (Part III of "Three Songs for Flannery O'Connor")

New Madrid: "The Consolation of Wind" and "Vigil"

Nimrod: International Journal of Poetry & Prose: "Somnambulance"

The North American Review: "Perspective"

Orion: "Dona Nobis Pacem"

Poet Lore: "Thoreau Hears the Last Warbler at the End of September"

Poetry East: "Thoreau Considers a Stone"

Quarterly West: "Thinking of Li Po while Fishing the Little J"

Rhubarb Magazine: "Begging Bowl," "Crow Counsels Me in the Ways of Love," "Offering, as One Example, the Satisfaction of the Bee" (as "The Waxen Comb of Delight"), and "Transfiguration"

River Styx: "What I Told My Sons after My Father Died"

Seminary Ridge Review: "Brushwolf"

Shenandoah: "The Girl Who Taught a Chicken to Walk Backwards" (Part I of "Three Songs for Flannery O'Connor")

Sou'wester: "The Gospel of Beauty"

Tar River Poetry: "Imago Dei" and "Umbilical"

Third Coast: "Hermetic"

Via Negativa: "Letter to Dave B. with May's Insatiable Hunger Tagging Along" and "Letter to Dave B. from the Karen Noonan Center on the Chesapeake Bay"

Water~Stone Review: "Meditation on Hunger at 2 A.M."

West Branch Wired: "A Consideration of the Word 'Home'" and "When the Body Is Absent"

"A Mennonite in the Garden" first appeared in the anthology, *Tongue Screws and Testimonies: Poems, Stories, and Essays Inspired by The Martyr's Mirror*, edited by Kirsten Beachy (Herald Press, 2010). "I'll Catch You Up" and "The Girl Who Taught a Chicken to Walk Backwards" were also featured on *Poetry Daily*.

Some of the poems in the second section of *In the Kingdom of the Ditch* appeared in a limited edition chapbook, *Household of Water, Moon, and Snow: The Thoreau Poems* (Seven Kitchens Press, 2010).

The epigraph by K. A. Hays is from "Migration" which originally appeared in *Dear Apocalypse* (Carnegie Mellon University Press, 2009).

Thanks to the following people for their encouragement and advice in the making of these poems and this book: Rick Bass, Martha Bates, Lori Bechtel-Wherry, Ervin Beck, Chris and Brian Black, Paula Bohince, Marcia and Bruce Bonta, Dave Bonta, David Budbill, Jim Daniels, Joyce and Harold Davis, Shelly Davis, Chris Dombrowski, David James Duncan, Don Flenar, Don and Punky Fox, Dan Gerber, K. A. Hays, William Heyen, Jane Hirshfield, Don and Melinda Lanham, Virginia Kasamis, Helen Kiklevich, Mary Linton, Carolyn Mahan, Ron Mohring, Dinty Moore, Erin Murphy, Mary Rose O'Reilley, Ben Percy, Lee Peterson, Jack Ridl, Dave Shumate, Michael Simms, Annette Tanner, Jack Troy, Patricia Jabbeh Wesley, and Ken Womack.

Many of these poems were finished with the help of generous grants from Pennsylvania State University.

ABOUT THE AUTHOR

Todd Davis is the author of four full-length collections of poetry—*In the Kingdom of the Ditch*, *The Least of These*, *Some Heaven*, and *Ripe*—as well as of a limited edition chapbook, *Household of Water, Moon, and Snow: The Thoreau Poems*. He edited the nonfiction collection, *Fast Break to Line Break: Poets on the Art of Basketball*, and co-edited *Making Poems: 40 Poems with Commentary by the Poets*. His poetry has been featured on the radio by Garrison Keillor on *The Writer's Almanac* and by Ted Kooser in his syndicated newspaper column *American Life in Poetry*. His poems have won the Gwendolyn Brooks Poetry Prize, have been nominated several times for the Pushcart Prize, and have appeared in such journals and magazines as *The American Poetry Review*, *The Iowa Review*, *Ecotone*, *The North American Review*, *Indiana Review*, *The Gettysburg Review*, *Shenandoah*, *Image*, *Orion*, *West Branch*, *River Styx*, *Poetry Daily*, *Quarterly West*, *Green Mountains Review*, *Sou'wester*, *Verse Daily*, and *Poetry East*. He teaches creative writing, American literature, and environmental studies at Pennsylvania State University's Altoona College.